Ann. 0872886892.
Farrell.

Girl   087 255 118.

AN ARID SEASON

Michael D. Higgins was born in Limerick on 18 April 1941 and reared in Newmarket-on-Fergus, Co. Clare. He studied at University College, Galway, Indiana University and Manchester University and has for many years lectured in Political Science and Sociology at University College, Galway. In 1992 he became the first recipient of the Seán McBride International Peace Medal of the International Peace Bureau for his work for human rights.

Michael D. Higgins is a Labour TD for Galway West and has twice been Mayor of Galway. From 1993 to 1997 he was Minister for Arts, Cultures & the Gaeltacht. He is currently Spokesperson on Foreign Affairs for The Labour Party.

His two previous collections were *The Betrayal*, published by Salmon, and *The Season of Fire*, published by Brandon, with drawings by Mick Mulcahy.

Michael D. Higgins' poetry has appeared in a number of anthologies and journals including *The Great Book of Ireland*, *The Leopardi Anthology*, *The Limerick Anthology*, *Fathers and Sons*, *Sons and Mothers*, *The Ogham Stone*, *The Wexford Anthology*, *The Irish Review*, *Céide* and anthologies published by The Dun Laoghaire Poetry Festival, UNICEF, Amnesty and Energy Action. He has read his poems on a number of radio and television programmes in Ireland and abroad.

AN ARID SEASON
new poems

MICHAEL D. HIGGINS

NEW ISLAND

AN ARID SEASON
First published 2004
by New Island
2 Brookside
Dundrum Road
Dublin 14
www.newisland.ie

ISBN 1 904301 57 6

British Library Cataloguing in Publication Data. A CIP catalogue record for this book is
available from the British Library.

Typeset by New Island
Cover design by New Island
Printed in Ireland by ColourBooks

New Island received financial assistance from
The Arts Council (An Chomhairle Ealaíon), Dublin, Ireland.

10 9 8 7 6 5 4 3 2 1

For Sabina, Alice-Mary, Michael, John Peter and Daniel who have given me so much, for all those from whom I have received the gift of friendship and particularly for those who continue to ask questions that might have answers that are not allowed.

Contents

ACKNOWLEDGEMENTS

Several of these poems were first published in anthologies or magazines. Acknowledgements are due to the editors of *The Whoseday Book, The Ogham Stone, Human Rights Have No Borders, Irish Writers against the War, Céide* and to the radio producers on whose programmes some of the poems have been read from time to time.

I would like to acknowledge the encouragement and assistance of the late Maureen Gordon, herself a poet, who typed some of these poems, Eileen Hayes, Judy Dunne, Noreen King and Michael Treacy, who had the patience to type some of the others many times, and Emma Dunne for her help. I would like to thank my son Michael for his editorial assistance and critical opinions on the final typescript. Ronan Sheehan was as generous as always in reading some of the poems for me. Mark Patrick Hederman and Ciarán Forbes provided encouragement, hospitality, humour and wisdom when I visited the Benedictine Community at Glenstal Abbey. I am grateful to the Abbot and all the members of the community for the shelter they provided under the Psalms.

STARDUST

It is of stardust we are
Moulded by vapours and fragments
From the making and breaking of galaxies.
We are the broken bits of our cosmos
Moved by traces of embedded memory,
Lurching always towards our image,
Of hopes unrealised and fading.
The promise of our as yet uncreated wholeness remains,
However weak.

From this flux we take refuge
In the cell of reason.
From that prison of categories
Our cry is heard
That we are not solely the children of reason

We have glimpsed the land of the heart.
The turbulence of present times recedes.
The stirring of that which is beyond
Time and space reverberates.

Our wonder invites us to make a journey
To stand against the false certainties
Of lesser tasks and poorer versions.

Out of exile our words will make
A plaintive discourse
That echoes of a lost prophecy.
Deep within we hear it call,
Offering more than a refuge,
Making a fresh story of a new time
And wondrous space,
A promise of the as yet uncreated joy,
Made out of stardust.

AN ARID SEASON

There is a darkness coming
That carries no moisture for a beckoning light.
It is a dry darkness that threatens
Of an arid time.

There are no words sufficient to rekindle a fire
Of the senses.

It is a silence
That greets the dark,
Where shadows of things past,
Flit past each other
Haunting memory
As breath shortens
In the lifeless time.

And in the airless time
A great sigh breaks.
Out of an endless longing
It aches for a new beginning,
For a word,
For love,
For hope.

When the silence breaks
Screams fill the air
And quiet prayers too
Directed at a God
Who remains as silent as a blasted oak.
Screams and prayers draw no answer
From the dry air.

And in that time inescapable
When planets die

There will be no sign
Of an old time of words.
All will have returned
To a dust
From which they came.

In these moments of half light
We should not be afraid to weep
At the coming darkness.

And from that moisture of tears
Will spring the vivid flashes
Of the senses
That allow us to dream
Of a shared space of humanity
In the time allowed.

It will come to be that in the shadows
The breathless ones
Will search for each other
Weeping for the lost words of love
Not formed in the time of changing seasons.
Making an unbearable sadness
In the inescapable darkness.

But in the half light let us sing
In celebration
And weep too
In honesty
For those lost words
Not formed,
The love not ripened,
The withered palm
Not held or kissed.

We are waiting between seasons.
The arid time beckons

And the beauty of the ordinary
Becomes precious.
No flowers bloom
As we gaze in wonder at a weed.

For in the roots of weeds now respected
In our wait between seasons
Are lodged no mere dust
But seeds of beauty
Scattered on the thin soil
Of hope that might survive
The airless time.

And no one knows
If it will ever be told,
Nor will it matter,
In infinite space
That we tried to make a story
With arrogant reason
In unbroken time.

That in the end
We yearned for hope
And a new place
Of spirit breath.

That in the place of spirit
New life might come again
To play a new game
With minds and words.
That is our prayer
On the edge of darkness.

It is no void
But a space of infinite love
That waits
Beyond the darkness.

Our final prayer
Is poured
Into the
Welcoming silence.

In the Beginning 1

In the beginning was the Word
But the Word was not the beginning.
When the light faded
On the gestures of order
Fired at unbroken time
The pieces descending
Into darkness
Did not arrange themselves
Except in arbitrary shape.

Nor was the beginning out of order.
Nor was the word that sought order the beginning.
The word was an arbitrary shape
Beyond gaze and breath.
It was in glorious darkness
Out of Chaos
The Word came.

That first scream of need
Is the beginning
Of a long surrender
That is not easily borne.
The struggle for a recovered silence
Will never be complete.
That look that precedes the word
Will stay to haunt.
The breath that interceded
Will break forth at times
In a great scream of grief or love.

And, if in weakness
We polish the wild words
To make a prayerful set of beads
From the jagged edges of stony times,

Or cry out on a Sunday shadow sated,
Then sing our souls
Not for the fading of the light
Nor yet the ebbing sea.
Through tears,
It is a worn face.
Not white
But ebony,
We seek
Calling from the darkness
Before the Word
And the false promise of order.

The salt of tears
Is a deposit in memory
Of our sea beginnings.
There is lodged
The long sigh
Of all our time
Lost in endless space.

In the Beginning 2

Breath and lungs conspire
Against the soul silence
For the hegemony
Of sound.

It is not just the words.
All accent is a form of falling further
Away from the breath space
That intercedes for a moment
Before capitulation
To the gasp of pain beginnings
In the gaze of the other.

And the words flow forth
Never ending in a long journey
Towards an exit
Resisted and unchosen.

We are condemned to rehearse
The memory of options not taken.
Over and over we turn the scruples.
They tear us apart,
Rendering impotent the generation
Of our needed new sensations,
The stuff of new beginnings.

Those lost moments crystallise
In memory
Making a reproach
That regularly obtrudes
In every present sensation,
Making an inexorable list
Of questions
Of reproach
Of loss sensation.

And together,
Why did we not look at stars
And grieve together
Or cry out and sing,
Or wade in water
Under the moon.

It can never be discarded
We are instructed,
That burden inherited,
Acquired from reflection
Of the gaze of the other.
We must perish we are told,
Locked in certainties
Not of our crafting,
In the silence of a misery
Circumscribed by the I.

Searching for prophecy
We make a song
Out of our exile
in the prison of the self.
We breathe again and assert
That nothing is inevitable.
It is no mere illusion
For which we struggle.
The making of a new world beckons.

The light that comes again,
In the dark chaos of words astray,
Promises a healing,
Invites towards the building
Of a new shared place
Of silence
Where nothing threatens.

In the Forest 1

Making my way into the forest
I move along paths,
Made personal
By sandalled feet
And barefoot intellect.

There where monks walk,
Traces of mind and spirit excursions
Hover,
And are dispelled
By a sudden new wonder
In a strange place,
Made personal by curiosity.

This is where the senses converge.
They do not debate
The constituent parts of moss.
They stretch to hear the question
Brought to the forest.

In those threatening moments of doubt,
When fear reverberates
Beyond sense silence,
A thought of light lost
Brings a cold sweat,
Defines the space
Beneath the canopy
Of lost growth.

The twisted failure of the half grown
Is everywhere,
Mouldering to the centre
From rotting bark.
Underfoot the leaves

Halfway to slime
Make a mottled shroud
Of decay.

But if at other times the question
Comes from an open heart,
It is the light undefeated
By the brash growth
Of a few seasons
That prevails.
The senses celebrate
In reminder forever
Of that space of transience,
Of Hero's secret wish
That Leander would never leave
The tent of passion
Made by artifice
For pleasure.

The visit to a moist place
Takes courage.
It could go either way.
Beyond the edge of remembered space,
Before the assurance of any tale,
The urge to pray overwhelms.
But even in the kneeling,
A magnet draws to danger,
Making out of pious necessity
The shape of an enduring scruple.

But if the gaze is up
The light may bring a miracle
Through the canopy of growth.
A shaft of light
Distils a beauty,
Dispels all shadow shapes and fears.
From the warm ooze

Of feeding life
I lift my feet
Towards the blinding light
Of the ordinary
Made safe.

In the Forest 2

On my way from the forest
Beyond the memory of gravel
And the blinding sun
I move with all my marks of bark
And twisted branch.

I do not ask
If mind can be prepared
As limbs
Dragged free
Beyond the wiping
Are coldly cleaned
For appearance.

That cleaning
Not an act for darkness
But for the crippling light of day
When flesh without a mark
Shines bright
Offering a limb without a story
Making a statement
Of scrubbed innocence.

I choose to keep my marks,
My dirt traces,
That cannot be erased,
My testament
Not for the forgetting,
For the remembering.

In memory is lodged more than the forest,
More than the crunch of gravel underfoot,
Or the feel of polished wood
In a country church

The spirit made light
In the holy dark
Through mutterings
Suffused with smells
Amid the dust and sweat
Of a wooden kiosk of contrition.

Out in the air
The sun dazzles
But does not blind,
Everything made clear.
For a moment my heart dances again.
It is no fiction of the mind,
No artful contrivance of innocence,
This surge of spirit
Makes a prophecy
Of hope recovered.

MEMORY

'And as Ricouer said,
To be removed from memory
Is to die twice.'
Nor should it be allowed
To make an amnesia
Of violence.
An amnesty is enough
For the detail.
And who knows whether,
If in time,
Such a healing is possible
As would make an evening
Of forgiveness
Worth the going on.
We make an affirmation.
The stuff of hope beckons.
Out of the darkness
We step,
And blink into the new light.

My Mother Married My Father in Mount Melleray in 1937

My mother married my father in Mount Melleray in 1937.

Those photos were the most precious
From before.
She in slight profile
Her best side
He fresh and determined
A strong face they said.
She wore her leather coat
For the going away
And he a blue grey jacket
In its lapel a badge
Given as a gift
Among many blessings
By the monk who performed the ceremony

My mother married my father in Mount Melleray in 1937.

Why should we not weep
And make the salt
For other tears
That teach to grieve
And source the long sigh
That breaks
Out of breath shaken
From the spirit
That trembles in its search
For truth

The remembered humiliation
The sharing of another's loss
Suggest a press of tears
That is too far from the heart

Distant from the source
That might connect the long sigh
To the wound deep
In interrupted breath.
I weep for the lost child
Not allowed by times
Made adult too soon
To gaze at joy exchanged,
Hear words bartered
In laughter.
It is the little things
That make a resonance
For certain
In oblique constancy
Lodged in creviced memory.
They hold on
And blossom.

My mother married my father in Mount Melleray in 1937.

On the side of a stony mill
My father
Going away again
An exotic visitor
Tells me he will walk the remaining mile alone
To a bus that will pause in front of the familiar
Withering cabbage plants in bundles
Forks and rakes in pristine cleanliness.
As we turn from each other
I place my frail hope
In his surviving energy.
From the warmth of his jacket lapel
He takes a badge
Worn since his marriage

My mother married my father in Mount Melleray in 1937.

It is an old indented badge
Moulded for the pushing through
And the anchoring
Not temporary
Image enamelled
Of a cross and hand
With reds and greens I cannot now distribute
Sign of a confraternity
A special membership
Something stubborn
Intimate
That had migrated with him
In his despair.

From lapel of once sturdy jacket
In fashion
Chosen for discretion in celebration
To the familiar coat
Of frayed intimacies
Now worn for warmth
In the necessity of his visit
To us his children
That he had already half lost
Its leathered cuffs asserting
A dignity of craft,
Perhaps a prudence,
He takes it.

My mother married my father in Mount Melleray in 1937.
No coins left nothing to give
He takes it from his coat
The badge more precious
Upon which my eyes had feasted
In his proximity.
He offers this gift in a hand I never kissed.
I kept it with me
And lost it in my own migrations.

When I remember now
This sacred little thing
I want to grieve for him
And let his anger go
And my childish shame.

My mother married my father in Mount Melleray in 1937.

I kept this secret gift
Of my father
In the space shared
Between us.
In a world of shortening time
Why is it not allowed to remember?
Why is it required to forego
Small and sacred moments
Scarce and precious things
From the spaces of between
Those iceberg times of forbidden touch
The slightest sign of tears
And love?

My mother married my father in Mount Melleray in 1937.

Even through grief
The healing is uncertain.
For all belief is thin belief
But little things can lodge
On a fragile surface.
Create a boundless aura
That enables the memory
To make a miracle.

My mother married my father in Mount Melleray in 1937.

THE WELL 1

It is not the well overgrown in excess
That lodges in the mind,
It is the one that has endured
In a dry season,
Defying prediction
Of an impending disaster,
Of drought
And cattle lost
To a dry season.

The soil dried, caked and cracked
By an unforgiving Sun
Is all around.
At the moist heart of the well
The mud defeated
By every past clearing of the water
Attempts a new statement
Of its victory at last.

Hardening its seal,
It waits
Until again a trickle appears
Of a spring from unknown depths
And source.
Makes its way
To the surface,
Announcing a renewal,
And the defeat of a dry season.

THE WELL 2

To visit again the well of friendship,
And draw on the end of an old rope
The bucket of one's life,
To listen as it clatters
Against the sides,
Making a rattling resonance of childhood,
Is the stuff of pilgrimage.
To make the long haul back
For a sweet drink
From a decrepit vessel
Binds up time.
Water hidden under the earth emerges
And makes a renewal.
The deep drink forges an old unity
Beyond all uncertainty.

SENSE MEMORY

The sense memory stored
Waits for a new function,
Kicking an old can,
The child admonished
By an amnesiac authority
That curtails his wonder,
Forgets it had a function once.
The child gives it a new life
With string
Or a kick.

The pouched sense memory
Thrown in to make a line
Waits for the spirit surge,
To give it new life
With a sigh
Or a kick.
Without the benefit of authority.

THE ASS

I recall the soft velvet of his ears,
As he bent in habit
For the winkers,
The resignation too of his
Taking the bit
Past the surrender of his yellow teeth.

The cross upon his back conferred
No sacred status,
More a reminder of a burden carried,
Nor did it guarantee
The paring of his hooves.

The head of an ass,
The warm udder of a cow,
The arrogant snort of a horse,
The exhausted pant of a dog,
The sharp cuts of a green fern,
The precarious blue of a bog iris,
The wonder of stranded eels,
The rush of water in gully and ditch.
What is it of these images that makes them endure
Past a time of catastrophe
The slow of death of a house
Where the thatch has given in?
It is a special intimacy perhaps,
Allowed in fields,
That lodges them as seed
In memory.

On those rare occasions when he broke
From trot to gallop
I soared with him past order,
Before the tug on the reins.

And I never hurried at the untackling,
Nor did I begrudge him
His freedom recovered.

More than an image lost
It is a companion
I seek
To recover.

THE OPENING OF THE CASE

Among the rituals of return
The opening of the case
By a figure dressed in black
Come home
From a far place,
Administering wonder,
Had its special space
Of licensed piracy.

Delivering magic in parcels,
Unpredictable shapes
Of the unexpected,
And in their midst
From the unveilings come
Pieces made human,
Carrying an inscription
Of shapes local,
Mythical and significant
In their own space.

From them shines
A glaze of mystery,
Line, myth and memory drawn
From the touch of older things.
Defining,
Signifying,
Something lodged deep beneath,
The skin of hands made busy in the crafting
Of a distant child's wonder.

That gift for adults made childish
In expectation
Was never an ornament merely.
From the indeterminate secret places

It came,
Was made ready for the packing,
And its revelation
In the opening of the case
Was a gift of wonder.

The gifts in their gathering
For the future scattering
Had become
But temporary possessions,
Placed with others
To jostle in a case
Itself a hoard,
Vessels filled with story
For the journey home,

Just ready,
For the migrant's return.

After the distribution,
Something of you had moved
Between us
And two places
Two times
Of your life
Your departures
And your returns
Had merged
In the circle
Of your migration.

When you closed the case
We knew in our hearts
That for you,
It was not the full story.
For that too
We were grateful.

Nocturne 1

The sick grey feeling
Of despair
Lodges in the stomach
Short of a great loss
That might release
A long sigh
It remains.
A dark shadow
Over my whole being.

Mind generated hope
Is insufficient
For its dislodgement.
This sickness of spirit
So long embedded.
Spirit does not answer
In these barren times.

Is it not a messenger of death that comes
With practised stealth
Laying down its long spectre
From drying skin
To memory's flight?

I would cry out in joy,
I would remember,
I would feel,
If only spirit answered
If only spirit showed itself
Even in shadow.

In the arid times
I miss its promised legacy.
Little bits glimmer and fade

Of that false expectation.
It is no autumn
Or harsh winter
Sustained by a promise
Of spring
That now threatens.
A final emptiness
And all before
A confusion
Of intensity
Without meaning
Without energy
Without hope.

But if the small and shimmering pieces hold
Just for a moment,
Just sufficient
To feed the curious
Onlookers
Whose time has not yet come,
Is it not enough
To have made a question?
More honourable
Than any expectation,
To hope
That from the question
Life might pause,
Allow the feeling
For the space
Of a tentative answer?
Quite enough
For the going on.
Quite enough
For the going out.

FACE TO THE WALL

When birds die,
Beak on bone,
All flesh wasted,
It is under the wing
That the head turns.

Sustained only
By the solitary warmth
Of the fickle down
They wait for the stiffening.

Children gone,
Hope abandoned,
Seed scattered,
In the dry time beyond tears,
It is away from the lamp
Before the Sacred Heart,
Face to the wall,
His head turns.

Face to the wall,
Head buried in a moist blanket,
Of guilt,
The fluff of memory
Floats in a shaft of winter sun,
Intangible.

Face to the wall they found him
A full fortnight after,
A neighbour's concern
Knocked on the door
Of the lonely place he waited
For the stiffening.
Bird and man

Of the same being
Take the last gasp alone
Before the journey back
To the sea beginning,
Where all is quiet,
And infinite.

Nocturne 2

The moth now feeble
That flung its wings
With passion
Against the burning lamp
Lingers,
With feeble gestures
On a sill
Among dust
Discarded.
Lonely in its last
Weak beat
Of Death.

THE GRIEVING

I have been grieving for the soft words
That passed this way
On whom I have shut the door
In this new place.

In solitary silence
I await the uninvited
Words of hate
Sharpened
On the venom stone.
I knew other words once
That shone from the polishing
Of love
And, even if in dream
As figments that flitted past
Evaporating
In light,
They gave me life.

At times,
I am afraid
That there will never be again
A space for the grieving.
If the soft words call again,
I will take them in.

In Gratitude

I lift the postcards, one by one,
Groping for more than the greeting,
For light in a dark place,
Confused,
Without the solace of words
In a silence not chosen,
Imposed,
In a time made barren
With singular labels.
I read the message
From the heart of a friend.
"Under the wall, the poet lives again
And Jara sings for you.
In the dark wood
The snowdrops are waiting for you."
My heart leaps
In gratitude,
And I see again the magic word,
"Love".
Oh, fellow poet,
I take your hand
And know
The stepping stones are safe.

REVIVALISTS

At the meeting some decided
That for the Revival
They would not have sex
Except for procreation,
With eyes averted.
Others were in favour
Of lots of it,
To build an army
For the Revival.

At any other business
After the nasty exchanges
About the true structure of grammar,
A Civil Servant with glasses demanded the floor.
"I know I'm stepping out of line,"
He blushed as he said it,
"But I want to talk of knickers
And long johns."

Some were shocked,
They spilled their balls of malt.
"They should be made of tweed," he said,
"Until the Revival is complete.
To remind us through the scratching
That we are suffering
For the Revival."

The numbed silence gave away
And the sound of cheers broke
Up from the basement
Out onto Molesworth Street
Where the crowd had gathered.
"They've gone for the tweed knickers,"

The whispers ran like wild fire,
"For the Revival."

The Guards who'd all changed their names,
Thousands of Civil Servants,
Members of Semi-State bodies,
Professors and eccentric Clerics,
That were gathered in Kildare Street
Danced a set together
In celebration.

Dancing outside their very own Dáil
They felt rightly proud.
They were making history.
The new nation had taken a decision
For the Revival
And they shouldered high
The man with glasses
Who dreamed the dream
And made the motion
Under any other business
That made it possible for them all
To wear tweed knickers
And scratch
For the Revival.

GOODBYE MR MICHAEL

On a night in Ammasaya
Necklaced with the tombs
Of the memorable,
Pockmarked in stone;
The Mayor was lamenting,
To me his subversive visitor,
That the old days were gone.

Time was
They would kill a pig each year,
They had meat
Once a year.
The Mayor was lamenting.

And earlier that day,
At lunch, the Prosecutor was citing
Crimes against the Turkish Constitution.
From Red Fatsa
He was demanding
Two hundred and fifty-nine death sentences.

Carrying a bag at night,
Fighting for the shoe polishing in the morning
With competitive brothers,
Little Fikri said
Goodbye Mr Michael.

On television
General Evren spoke for the length of two episodes of *Dallas*;
In the Hotel I was packing again,
For my return home.

THE CROSSING

Across the stream in his need
I see my friend at the other side.
I would cross over.
I place stones in the water.
They disappear in insufficiency.
I take the larger ones and struggle
To make a path to our union.

I feel his isolation where he waits.
The bridge of my anxiety distracts,
Of no value in the task of reconciliation.
I cannot know
The nature of his waiting.

I bend to the task and continue
With no certainty
Only conviction
That the stones
Must be made safe.

Lone Diner on Koh Samet

(For Paddy Leahy)

He sits alone at tables
In exception.
A fantasy loner
Eating fried rice
Among the accompanied
The beautiful
The validated.

In the slow evenings
Of the New Year
Even the older man
Alone
Holds on
In the humid warmth
To the cheerful overflow
Of back-pack intimacies.

Late night children
Indulged
In the hearing of parents and the sea
Make their own stories.

The stories,
The children,
The full moon on Koh Samet
Give an artificial strength
Of understanding.
Watching the tide go out
Waiting for its return
Firing finite thoughts
At infinity
And the high tide
In Koh Samet.

He weeps for things lost
And moments left empty
Of love.

The years slip away
In the swell,
Their return
More than one tide away,
Giving only an assurance
Of questions without answers
Endless,
And all around the sounds of laughter
Needing no answers
For the moment
Under the full moon of Koh Samet.

OLD WADERS ON KOH SAMET

There is a secret transcript
That men share
In prostate years.
They rehearse the leaving of their bodies
For sense travel.

They try to board that bamboo raft of sensation
From which the laughter of the young
Rings out
Making a nebulous attraction.

Wading out into the water
Of memory,
With excess baggage of flesh and feeling
These old men flounder.
More slowly they turn.
As they make it back
It is the coiled rope
They see,
Dry on the pier
At one time useful.

THE RAFT

(For Daniel)

The broken wood has drifted
On to the lonely beach they visit.
In collusion
They have made this space.
Between moments stolen
From a life prescribed.

The materials discarded beckon,
Have drifted
From a narrow function.
They carry but traces of their past.

A child envisages a raft
Made from the useless flotsam,
In such time as may be allowed,
On which to embark upon a journey
For which there is no map.
He makes a preliminary question.
His father tells him
It is time to go home.

The shared moment is over.
Turning their backs to the sea
They drive
Away from wonder
Father and Son
In silence.

On the shore the broken bits remain,
Waiting for the sea
To make its new demands.
At night the child dreams
Of a raft rising and falling

With the waves.
In sleep he visits again
The lonely beach,
And vows to make a return,
To try again.
His father turns out the light.

POL POT IN ANLON VENG

In the *Bangkok Post*
Pol Pot is breaking his silence.
From Anlon Veng
He does not reminisce
Of millions of piled skulls,
No nightmare image
From the killing fields
Obtrudes.

He is finished
He says
With politics.

He is a nationalist still
Who has conviction
And time left
To hate Vietnam.
When regret might be expected
He announces
He is ill.
He tells the *Bangkok Post* he is dying.

Waiting for death
Unlike the millions
Who fed a monster's dream.
In polite space
He is interviewed.

On its front page
The *Bangkok Post* tells us
That the Baht is in free fall,
That an American President
Has called from Airforce One
To assure us
That he loved Thailand.

MEETING

Beneath
The blackness of a bog
Reduced to soup,
Beyond
The side of a mountain
Made bare,
Lies an old violence
Against nature.
Sustained with a sneer,
Hushed with a cuteness
That offers solidarity
In the covert greed
Of Gombeen mutterings.

You are right to make your demand.
Do what you like with it
As your fathers did before you.
That few inches of soil
Are all you have.
Who are all these strangers?
Are we not here for generations?
He had them now.
He could let go.
Banging the side of a car
With an ash plant
Was the best way
To drive the cattle
As your fathers did before you.
He was sucking diesel.

Hard faced and cold,
He smiled at his own words.
They resonated.
He knew he had them.

Fuck the ecology,
They roared.

Going home he felt certain
They would be his forever.

THE MADMAN'S VISITOR

He was gazing at the flowers
When she came,
His first visitor
In twenty years.

Past the fragrant nuns she moved
Defeating the cacophony of their metal bowls,
A symphony in duty
To the God
For whom they starched their headdresses
And sterilised their instruments.
At a distance
They slyly squinted
At her loveliness,
His first visitor
In twenty years.

"I know your story," she said
To the man who never had a visitor.
"I think it's very moving," she said.
The torrent of words refreshed the room.

But in just a little while
She stopped.
And when she spoke again
He heard the words.
They all heard the words.
"I must fly," she said,
His first visitor in twenty years.
He looked up
In a way that frightened her.
"I must swim," he said,
The man who never had a visitor.

THE WINCHMAN

The creaking of the winch is regular.
From the corner of the tent,
His testing pull of the wire
Is achieved with singular intent.
His gaze as she steps tentatively
On the high wire
Is unbroken.
The keeper of her safety
In a solitary task
It is not to him she turns.
It is the audience that needs her smile
Crafted out of danger.
At the man who tends the wire
They never gaze.
Content in their disinterest
He is singular in his task.
She balancing with a pole
Is making a performance.
To a minor role the audience consigns him.
They only know the half of it.

THE BOWL

It is the bowl I touch,
Both hands lifting,
In exception
To the single movements
All around.
An amateur
In a communion
Of profession,
In silence.

VOICES AT EVENING

The company of voices at evening
Is a sweetness asserted
Against a cloying silence
Of nature,
A struggle from the chasm
Of the sun's exit
In darkness.
Against the waiting for the light,
The giddy sounds
Make their own statement
Of humour,
The mark of our transience
Where lightly covered
Lies the hope
Of our humanity
And a new day.

Nocturne 4

In a space cluttered
With times burden
Of story and place,
It is easy to conclude
That there is no escape
From the given,
That allowed,
Tolerated.

A sliver of light
Makes a reminder,
Offers a prospect of hope
And times defeat,
Hinting of a place not yet reached
Where the spirit flies
Past minds weary of capitulation.

In the darkness
A smile breaks
On the prisoner's face.
Time and space defeated,
A life without burden beckons,
Night recedes,
Makes way
For a new day,
Different,
Not yet born.

The Sense-Voices of Spirit

The spirit shines on the lurking grief
Pushing sorrow out
Beyond the edge
Of Time and Space.
Dissolved
It fades
In the void
Of light.

EXILES

No it is not the end of history.
Nor is it a possibility exhausted,
Not yet the end of ideas.
It is the time of a single idea,
Crippling, vicious and deadly,
Closing us off
From what we imagined of a world
We have not yet managed to create,
Rejecting the possibility
Of hope,
Of a better version of ourselves

And in the new intolerance
We may not speak of prophecy.
We may not make a criticism
Of the choices made
In our name.
The mind of war is being remade,
New demons invented,
And language gives way
To description
Of demons.
A picture is being drawn
Of those less than human who differ.

An old vision of freedom
From hunger, fear, abuse,
Has faded in the terrible times.
We are invited to forget an old promise
That ours was a world to create.

Out of the depths we cry.
We shrink in fear.
Few break the silence.

But then light flickers
In hope,
In resolution.

We must make our own answer.
Our liberation from the nightmare will come.
Our exile will end,
Not from the making of miracles
But from the strength of will and heart combined,
Affirming
That we make our own history
With heart and head.
We make our common fate.
Together
We move on and recall
That old promise,
Not rejected,
Unfulfilled.

UNDER THE MANGO TREE

When they gather under the Mango Tree
It is of survival they dream.
There is no long past,
No victories jog the senses
Nor can memory recall either
A moment of defeat.

HORSESHOE

Out of proportion,
In the half darkness,
The blows fall,
Making sparks
From the molten magic.

Earth, fire and water
Combine in the strike
Of hammer on iron,
To make a shape
That arrives glowing
Held to the light
Only needing the space for nails,
A shining creation
That makes the badge of another's service.

On to the hoof the nails are driven
With certainty.
The rasp is last,
Making smooth the transition to work
With winkers and chains.
On leaving the horse beats the road tenderly,
And who could decide
If it were music
Or just a sign
Of a life made useful.

And at the end on grass,
No new miracle
Of the dark or sweat
Is needed to make a shape
Beyond the use of man.
The horse snorts,
In a brief freedom,

At one with earth and stone,
His hooves feel the freedom earned,
Unshod,
After a life prescribed.

TOO CLOSE TO THE GROUND

Too close to the ground
Our gaze was downwards
At the wet drill,
At the hooves of cattle
Eyes raised only to their backs,
Driven before us to fairs,
Where we competed for mute subjection.

Too close to the ground
For sunsets,
And landlord seasons,
Making the sounds horses knew
For the pulling of the plough
Was a man's work.
Women making sounds
For ducks and geese,
That was our lot for language.

The gaze was never upwards.
To the sun we were indifferent,
At its going up and coming down
Others marvelled.

Our children's children
Talk of scenery
And the body
And the sea.
Too late for us.

Too close to the ground
There were so many of us
And we heard that some
In Africa after the toil of day
Forgot the heat and in the cool of night

Took signs from Sirius
And colours of lilac and orange
And black with shards of gold.

Heart and head are needed
In the raising of the head to the sun.
And in that action our world moans.
Waiting to be born it cries out,
And we are reminded
That we make our own hope and history.

Making a New Season

To stretch,
That was always the issue,
Beyond the limit
Of the prescribed
Inevitable.
To draw the spirit breath,
That was the challenge,
That made the big questions.
The children with swollen stomachs,
The women excluded,
The science distorted
For war,
The bombs preferred to bread,
Are not inevitable.
The child made homeless
Learned from his mother,
His father and a donkey
That this was so,
That someone must go to the Temple,
Should question
What was not inevitable.
And he never claimed
That he was alone
In such a view.
Just that Bethlehem mattered,
In memory,
And that spirit breath suggested
That we make a new life
Where spirit shone through pain
And death,
Making a prophecy,
For ever,
Empowering,
Promising a joy,

Not confined to any season.
Beyond the inevitable.
Our hope makes possible
A new season,
In a different world,
Waiting for our creation.
Utopia regained.

SPIRIT FLIGHT

It is alone that Spirit flies.
There is no joining of hands,
No dance,
Or any sigh at what is left
On Earth.

No memory of that time
When flesh and spirit fused,
In the small space
Of life,
Prevails.

And will it search for companions?
Will it call out?
Or answer?
Only the uncertainty
Is confirmed.

The Crafting

It is the craft of the delivery that has escaped us.
That knowledge poured through the senses
Makes an accretion,
Leads to a wisdom
That is patient
In its waiting for us.
Beyond our mapmaking
And the search for coordinates,
It makes manifest
That which is waiting
For emergence.

The truth when it emerges
Will not be judged by categories
Of remembered sensation,
Nor yet by clever precepts.
It shall not make an obsession
Nor will it recall a scruple.

This sacred craft
An invocation,
Of our completeness
A celebration,
That makes of vulnerability
A heroic journey,
Offers a resolution
In joy.

We are not called to imitate.
We are the creators
Free to tell the whole story.

This crafting of the truth
Demands that in the task

We must reveal
Much that is hidden,
Requires that we walk naked
Along paths of memory,
Through disappointing alleys
Of the imagination,
Comforted only
That on our journey
We are not alone.
No longer afraid
We laugh along the way.
That is our strength
Revealed.

CONVERSATIONS

(For Alice Mary)

Let's have conversations
Instead of advice.
Let's have conversations
Instead of rows.

I look at this plant
That needs the light
And curse the jumble of darkness
That intervenes
Between my daughter's love
And my words.